Two very unusual animals stand in the distance.

W9-BTR-479

It is a mother giraffe and her baby.
She is called
a cow. Her baby
is a calf.
Here and there,
other giraffes graze quietly.

WILD ONES

GIRAFFES

by JI...

CORNING PUBLIC LIBRARY

603 9TH ST.

CORNING, IA 50841

(641) 322-3866

NorthWord
Minnetonka, Minnesota

...ng
...s
of Africa.

Look

at

their

l-o-o-o-ong

necks!

They have
very long
legs, too.
They stand
on hard feet
called hooves,
which can
be as big as
a dinner plate.

The only parts of
a giraffe that aren't
super-sized are the
mane of short, stiff
hairs on its neck and
the two stubby horns
between its ears.

With such a long neck, the giraffe is built to be a leaf eater. It can reach treetops that no other animal can reach.

Its long, black tongue rips the leaves off the branches.

It is much harder for a giraffe to reach the ground. It must spread its front legs apart and

its neck just to get a drink of water.

When giraffes are not eating, they are chewing. A giraffe chews and swallows its food just like you do. Later on, the food makes the long trip back up its throat to be chewed some more.

When a calf is first born, its body isn't ready to nibble on leaves.

grow **big** and **strong.**

It needs its mother's milk to

This can be a real stretch for a small calf!

When the calf is a little older,
it plays around with other calves.
They chase and push each other
to see who's strongest. Their
mothers take turns babysitting.

If a mother giraffe senses danger, she tucks her baby underneath her.

One kick with her sharp hooves may kill a lion that gets too close.

As the sun sets, the giraffes' spotted coats blend in with the shadows.

Standing tall, they will rest until tomorrow comes.

For Alastriona,
the first baby I fell in love with
—J. A.

Composed in the United States of America
Designed by Lois A. Rainwater • Edited by Kristen McCurry

Text © 2005 by Jill Anderson

NORTHWORD
Books for Young Readers
11571 K-Tel Drive
Minnetonka, MN 55343
www.tnkidsbooks.com

All rights reserved. No part of this work covered by the copyrights herein may be reproduced or used in any form or by any means—graphic, electronic or mechanical, including photocopying, recording, and taping of information on storage and retrieval systems—without the prior written permission of the publisher.

Photographs © 2005 provided by:
Anup & Manoj Shah: cover, pp. 14, 18; Digital Vision/Punchstock.com: back cover, pp. 1, 9, 13, 19, 21;
Robin Brandt: endsheets, pp. 2-3; Brand X Pictures/Punchstock.com: pp. 5, 20;
Frans Lanting/2003 Minden Pictures: p. 6; Craig Brandt: pp. 7, 8, 15, 24;
Mitsuaki Iwago/2003 Minden Pictures: pp. 10-11; Garykramer.net: p. 12;
YVA Momatiuk/John Eastcott/Minden Pictures: p. 16; Photodisc/Punchstock.com: pp. 22-23.

Library of Congress Cataloging-in-Publication Data

Anderson, Jill.
Giraffes / by Jill Anderson.
p. cm. -- (Wild ones)
ISBN 1-55971-928-1 (hardcover) -- ISBN 1-55971-929-X (pbk.)
1. Giraffe--Juvenile literature. I. Title. II. Series.

QL737.U56A535 2005

599.638--dc22   2004031117

Printed in Malaysia
10 9 8 7 6 5 4 3 2 1